I0617374

Environmental Lifestyle Guide

For Grade 11 Students

VOL.6 OF 11

Stationery

Jahangir Asadi

Vancouver, BC CANADA

Published by: Silosa Consulting Group Inc.
Vancouver, BC **CANADA**
Email: Info@Silosa.ca
www.silosa.ca

Ordering Information:
Quantity sales. Special discounts are available on quantity purchases by universities, schools, corporations, associations, and others. For details, contact the "Sales Department" at the above mentioned email address.

Environmental lifestyle Guide Vol.6 for Grade.11/J.Asadi —1st ed.
ISBN: 978-1-990451-80-5

Contents

We hope that, 10,000 years from now, future generations
will be able to see flowers that provide bees with nectar
and pollen and...
BEES provide flowers with the means to reproduce by
spreading pollen from flower to flower,....

Jahangir Asadi

This book is dedicated to my professor, Dr.Bijan Esfandiari

Introduction

This book is part of an eleven volume series that is meant to be a standard textbook series, for grades 9 to 12. TTAIN & ESFK & SCG improves quality of life and reduces environmental degradation by fostering new consumption patterns and sustainable lifestyles through International Cooperative Extension Service programs at houses, offices, schools and libraries all over the globe.

Climate change is real. Therefore people have the potential to make a difference now and for future generations. This book provides climate science basics, including the roles that lifestyles and populations play in the climate scenario, the significance of carbon footprints, and an overview of the current climate situation. The manual has been categorized based on humanity's needs starting first with food and ending with tourism. The manual then illustrates the difference between adaptation (taking steps to live with the changes) and mitigation (taking steps to slow the rate of change.)

Adaptation examples include food, energy, transportation, recreation. Mitigation focuses on effectively engaging with local governments, through serving on advisory boards, communicating with public officials, educational institutes, schools, universities, libraries and leading communities towards climate change actions.

One useful way to mitigate climate change is through increasing public knowledge to better understand the impact of the rate of change on plants and animals. This is crucial for preserving species; and for assessing potential insects and disease outbreaks in agriculture, natural resources and public health.

Taking personal action is a key element of this manual.

Citizens are challenged to consume 20% fewer resources, to bring world consumption levels down as much as possible. Readers are given 12 practical steps to take to make the changes. The resources section provides additional information, and readers are encouraged to contact the author for further questions.

As an accessibility action, we have provided Online international courses on climate change control as well. You can access the courses via the following link:

http://TopTenAward.org

SILOSA Consulting Group (SCG)

Silosa Consulting Group (SCG) was established to provide outstanding consulting services of management system & educational standards to individuals, groups, companies, schools, and organizations all over the globe. SCG is publishing an "Environmental Lifestyle Guide " book series as a standard textbook related to increasing environmental awareness of students means being aware of the natural environment and making choices that benefit the earth, rather than hurt it. Vol.1 to 11 (for grades 9 to 12) providing some of the ways to practice environmental awareness include: **Recycling**, **Conserving energy and water**, **Reuse, Activism, and others**.

SCG book publishing services and distribution services are connected to over 39,000 booksellers worldwide, including Apple, Amazon, Barnes & Noble, Indigo, Google Play Books, and many more. SCG has enough experiences to help create new and effective environmental educational programmes in different countries all over the world. For more detail, visit our website : http://silosa.ca and/or send your enquirer to the following email:

info@silosa.ca

CHAPTER 1

About ISO 14000 for Students

The International Organization for Standardization is an independent, non-governmental organization, the members of which are the standards organizations of the 165 member countries. It is the world's largest developer of voluntary international standards and it facilitates world trade by providing common standards among nations. More than twenty thousand standards have been set, covering everything from manufactured products and technology to food safety, agriculture, and healthcare.

Kids ISO 14000s
"Kids ISO 14000s" is a new environmental education program for children, based on ISO 14000s, which is international standard for environmental management. Primary aims of this program are: -
1. To teach and train children how to manage the environmental issues (such as energy saving) by themselves through the working book and guide book of this program,
2. To certify those children who showed good accomplishment in the program from highly international authority (as is the case of ISO 14000s)
3. To network those children through the international network (Kids International Network), so that the children can work on the environment, internationally.

2. System of Kids ISO 14000s Program

The system of Kids ISO 14000s Program consists of

1. Operation Headquarter (ArTech).

2. Workbook, Guidebook (originally published by ArTech, and local versions are produced by each countries).

3. Eco-Kids-Instructors for local operation and evaluation of the performance of the children.

4. International accreditation committee for accreditation of accomplishment of the children, for certification of the Eco-Kids-Instructors, as well as overall checks of this program.

5. Linkage with international organizations (such as UNU, UNESCO, etc. …) And also national organizations

More information can be obtained :

www.ISO.org

Canada

Environmental Sustain for Future kids established in Vancouver, BC Canada in 2020. (ESFK) is an international ecolabel focused on taking care of environment for future of kids. ESFK defined as 'self-declared' environmental claims made by manufacturers and businesses based on ISO 14020 series of standards, the claimant can declare the environmental objectives and targets in relation to taking care of environment for future kids. However, this declaration will be verifiable.

Environmental Sustain for Future Kids
Vancouver, BC CANADA

Email: info@esfk.org
Web: www.esfk.org

CANADA SILVER BEAVER BADGE

Participate in our Online Classes to earn these exclusive digital badges!
www.toptenaward.org

Design & Development by:

Tara Asadi

All about 'Eco-friendly'
Wood & Stationery Products

E co-friendly stationery is a broad category that encompasses recycled and sustainable stationery, along with zero-waste gifts like eco-friendly notebooks that can be fully recycled once they have been used. The term applies to all kinds of green stationery, from eco-friendly pens and pencils, to recycled notebooks and ethical stationery gifts – and different products might have different ethical and environmental credentials. For example, some eco stationery may be made from ethically produced materials like sustainably managed timber, while others might use more recycled raw materials or be designed in such a way to avoid ending up in a landfill site.In this volume, we'll look in more detail at what makes green stationery 'green' and why it makes sense to buy eco-friendly stationery for yourself and others.

What is sustainable stationery?

There's no strict definition of sustainable stationery. It could be recycled or recyclable (or both), it might use raw materials that would otherwise go to landfill, or it might be ethical in some other way. Because it's such a broad definition, there's plenty of choice, allowing you to choose a sustainable pen that fits your lifestyle and your own eco priorities.

Why should I try sustainable stationery?

There's really nothing to lose. Sustainable stationery often does not cost any more than its traditional equivalents, and there are some really stunning designs of eco pens, pencils and notebooks to choose from.

YOU CAN MAKE A CONSCIOUS EFFORT TO BE ENVIRONMENTALLY FRIENDLY

If you want to take action for sustainable living, without making major changes to your lifestyle, eco stationery is a simple first step to take. Sustainable stationery products function exactly as normal and there's usually no visible difference either, so you get peace of mind without compromise.

IT SETS A GOOD EXAMPLE

As well as improving your personal eco-profile, you can encourage others to take their own action for sustainable living too. International Environmental Labelling Book series of 11 volumes is a great gift for this scenario; by giving it to friends, family and co-workers. You can give this book series (look at the end of this book for more detail), an eco-friendly notebook, pen or pencil and send them on their own path towards a more eco-friendly life-style.

YOU WILL REDUCE WASTE

Sustainable stationery is typically designed to last longer. In fact, any refillable pen will generate less waste than a disposable pen, so opt for a cartridge pen, traditional fountain pen or refillable ball pen if you want to do your bit.

If you are in business, you could consider giving a customised eco-friendly gift, to encourage your customers to cut down on their use of disposable stationery too.

How does eco-friendly stationery help the environment?

Eco-friendly stationery (depending on the product) can divert materials away from landfill during its manufacture, and reduce landfill waste due to disposable plastic pens being thrown away. Sustainable stationery is also more likely to use renewable raw materials such as wood and eco plastics, rather than single-use plastics made from fossil fuels.

How is sustainable stationery made?

Green stationery is made from sustainable raw materials – and these, in turn, are produced using ethical, long-term sustainable practices. For example, One of the the largest pencil brand in the world, has a pioneering forestation project in Brazil and Colombia where two million trees are planted every year. Whenever a tree is felled to provide timber for more than the 2.2 billion pencils manufactured each year, a new one is planted. This is just one example of how sustainable stationery can be made and managed.

Which sustainable stationery products should I try?

Ecolabel programs authorize the use of environmental logos on products or services that meet a strict set of criteria. These ecolabels indicate an overall environmental preferability of a product or service within a particular product or service category based on life cycle "considerations," although not necessarily a more complex full life cycle assessment. Some ecolabels are created and managed on a national level while others are international in scope. They may be administered by government bodies or private sector labelling standards organizations, and typically involve certification by legitimate and independent third party organizations.

Final thoughts

We could all live a little more sustainably, but simple steps like using more sustainable stationery allow us to do so without compromising on our existing lifestyles in any significant way. Many people have already swapped plastic drinking straws for metal, bamboo or paper equivalents. Switching to green stationery is an obvious next step. And with such a great selection of eco pens and pencils, eco-friendly notebooks and zero-waste gifts available, there's no reason to delay investing in a great-quality pen or pencil that will stay by your side for many years to come.

19 Eco Friendly And Zero Waste School Supplies

New stationery and school supplies has always been an exciting time for most kids (and many adults too!). Writing this article brings back memories of fresh stationery and the joys of organizing and reorganizing pens, pencils, rulers, notebooks…Although, for parents and adults who are aiming to keep school sustainable though, it can bring a sense of dread. Plastic packaging, toxic components, and boxes of unused junk. To help, here are a few strategies for sustainable, low or zero waste school supplies and stationery:

Use what you already have. Scrounge up loose pens and forgotten notebooks (they're usually full of mostly blank pages!).
For things you know you no longer need, consider donating any school supplies that still have a useful life and recycling those that don't.
See what you can find secondhand. eBay is a good place to look for secondhand online school supplies like books, graphing calculators, and other technology (now that many classrooms and home learning programs require tablets). For anything you weren't able to check off with the first two, opt for a zero waste online store or general ethical online shop for eco-friendly back to school supplies as an opportunity to start teaching your kids about conscious consumerism.

For items you end up having to buy new, this list of the best eco-friendly school supplies (including sustainable stationery) will hopefully help. We've tried to find at least one solid sustainable item to fill each major common item. Most of us need office supplies at some point or another, and the two categories are really all the same. So no matter how old you are, there's just as much reason to make sure your office (and school) supplies are eco-friendly.

1. Plantable Pencils

Sustainable FSC certified wooden pencils are zero waste and have a non-toxic natural clay and graphite core. Then, instead of an eraser, they're capped with a biodegradable seed capsule. When your pencil gets too stubby to write with, just stick it in some soil as per their planting guide. Use the crafting potential of these to teach your child some apartment gardening basics! Choose from plain graphite, colored pencils, and inscribed sets. The Mindful Thoughts edition, which bears phrases like "All of us need to grow continuously in our lives", might even help get those creative juices flowing.

2. Recycled Newspaper Pencils

If you're worried about your kids losing their pencils, another eco-friendly pencil alternative is "tree-free" recycled newspaper pencils. These HB soft graphite pencils are comprised entirely of recycled newspapers and magazines. No wood at all, and they look pretty to boot. With an easy peel-to-sharpen design, these are great for kids. Just make sure to help them compost the peels to be truly zero waste. Sets of 5 or 10 come packaged in compostable, unbleached paperboard boxes.

3. Bamboo Pencil sharpener

Sharpen your eco-friendly pencils with this double hole eco-friendly pencil sharpener made of sustainably sourced bamboo and recycled stainless steel. At the end of its life, remove the blades for recycling and compost the bamboo body. It comes packaged with an unbleached cardboard backing printed with soy inks. The only slight downside is the recycled (and recyclable) plastic bit that holds the sharpener inside. This means it's not totally zero waste, but it was the closest we found on the market.

4. Natural Eraser

The dual-sided eraser made of all-natural rubber latex (to erase pencil) and natural silica sand (to erase ink and some markers). One zero waste eraser for all your mistakes. The individual erasers are packaged in a protective, 100% recycled pulp sleeve, which can be composted. Avoid the multi-packs because those are bound together in plastic packages.

5. Natural Grass Pen

Zero waste pens still leave us drawing a bit of a blank. While more sustainable pens exist now, they're still largely wasteful and greenwashing is still a concern, too. The truly best zero waste pens are refillable fountain pens. Great for the office, but perhaps less so for the classroom. That said, you can pick up a fountain pen for a reasonable price and while not totally zero waste either, we feel it's still one of the best alternatives. A good balance of very low waste while still being affordable. If you look after them they'll last a very long time. And you can sometimes find great secondhand fountain pens to reduce your waste further. Otherwise A Natural Grass Pen is a good option for kids. Just remember to gather up all those pens lying around the house and/or office, and use them first. When you're done so they can be recycled!

6. Organic Cotton Pencil Case

Now you need something to store all those eco-conscious goodies in, If you don't have a ditty bag lying around the house check out this line of eco-friendly school supplies from Canada. Their 100% organic cotton zippered pencil bags are available in tons of colors. Each bag is handwoven by underprivileged women in rural area in different countries, so as to provide jobs to these communities. The thick, ultra durable weave is designed to last, even when it gets buried under books in a backpack.

7. Decomposition Books

The best sustainable notebooks we found are different type of Decomposition books. These lovely college-ruled decomposition books are an excellent non-toxic and compostable note-taking solution. Each page is made of 100% post-consumer recycled paper. With so many nature-inspired cover designs (which are printed using soy inks), you can get something different for each subject or mood. Producer also makes spiral-bound notebooks, though we suggest avoiding if possible. Spiral bindings are inherently more wasteful.

8. Jotter Notebooks

Simple and elegant, these 30% recycled notebooks bound with wax thread are good for both school, work, sketching, journaling, or just making lists. Choose between blank, lined, or 3mm grid dot sheets (which would be perfect as graphic paper for math class). These zero waste notebooks measure 5" x 7" and come with a choice of either 30 or 60 sheets. You can also order them either individually or in packs of three or six. After you're done with the notebook, you can compost the pages and plant the seed paper cover to grow wildflowers! The embedded seeds will grow a blend of Snapdragon, Bird's Eye, Black-Eyed Susan, Clarkia, Sweet Alyssum, and Catchfly.

9. Recycled ReBinder

An undyed zero waste binder is never going to be as cool as the Trapper Keepers you coveted as a kid. But the planet will thank you! No more synthetic fabric-covered or plastic binders (one of many types of plastic, which are lucky to last even a semester). These recycled chipboard ReBinders are a far more durable choice, with a better end of life when they do wear out. Easily screw out the rings for recycling and throw the rest in the compost! And you could even draw on your own designs!

With 0.5" rings, you can fit about 100 sheets of recycled loose leaf paper. Fortunately, that's now pretty easy to find at just about any major office supply store.

10. 2-Pocket Folder

Unbleached folders are made using 22-point chipboard, which is 100% recycled FSC-certified post-consumer waste. This material is thick and durable, eliminating the need for any toxic coatings, including acids that can harm papers. Plus, then your kid (or you for that matter) can decorate it as they like. They're sold in sets of 25 to minimize shipping and packaging.

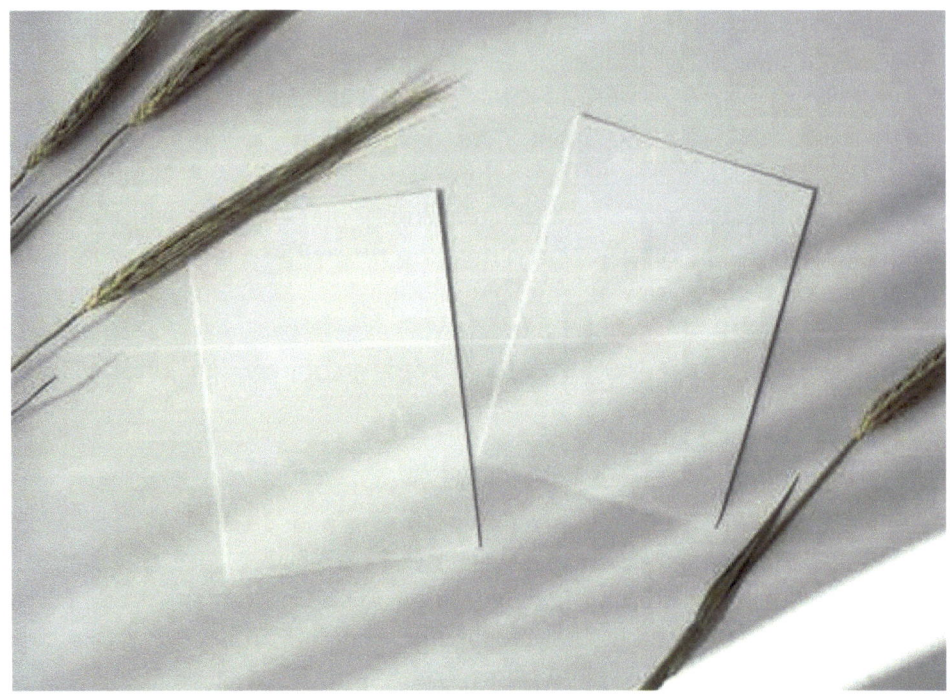

11. Recycled Tab Dividers

About Package Free Shop Recycled and Zero Waste Tab Dividers Your zero waste binder may help keep the planet clean, but how do you keep it clean and organized? With 3-ring compostable chipboard tab dividers, of course! These 5 or 8 tab sets are made out of 85% post-consumer and 15% post-industrial recycled content. With a 13-point thickness, they're durable and should last well beyond one school year. When they do wear out, you can home compost them.

12. Recycled Copy Paper

Not only is Printworks paper made of 100% recycled post-consumer waste (specifically from food and beverage containers), it's FSC-certified and chlorine-free. Unlike many recycled paper products that get shipped to Asia and back again, the waste is collected and remade entirely in the USA (only 300 miles from the mill, in fact). This reduces tons of carbon emissions from shipping. And since it comes in 20-pound boxes, you won't be needing to reorder anytime soon, either. It's just as affordable as traditional copy paper, too. We shouldn't have to choose between paying ourselves and making the planet pay.

13. Staple-Free Stapler

We don't have to prick our fingers pulling out staples before composting or recycling anymore? The PLUS Paper Clinch uses a unique folding technique to bind up to 10 sheets of paper just as staples would… but without all the waste and complication. It's also portable, kid-safe, and, according to the reviews, easy to use due to the ergonomic design and minimal force required. Unfortunately, the body is plastic,but if you take care to make it last, you're at least saving the staples and making whatever you're stapling easier to compost!

14. Paper Tape Cuts

Lasting Things paper tape cuts are made from upcycled 1970s vintage military surplus kraft paper combined with all-natural, compostable acacia gum. To activate the adhesive, just moisten a little bit and stick where desired. While this brown tape may not have all the advantages of clear tape, the biodegradable cello tapes can't be home composted. Besides, the kraft paper look gives it all sorts of crafty potential especially if used in combination with zero waste gift wrapping. An order includes 97 cuts of 9" x 2.5" sizes.

15. Eco-Friendly Backpacks

What good are eco friendly school supplies without a way to tote them? When it comes to something that takes quite a beating like a backpack, true quality is what you want, even more than sustainable materials. United By Blue offers tons of affordable eco friendly backpacks that are both. Their also are made of natural materials like organic waxed cotton canvas, or vegetable dyed repreve recycled polyester. With double stitching and DWR finishes, these are designed to last. They have many designs and sizes, many with internal laptop sleeves to function as two items in one.

16. Cork Laptop Sleeve

This minimalist, zero waste and vegan laptop sleeve is a great way to protect your hardware in your bag or on your commute. The cork provides some padding and water resistance while the cotton liner protects from scratches. But what is cork fabric? It happens to be one of the world's most sustainable materials because it's harvested by shaving the bark of cork trees, as opposed to cutting them down. This process can be repeated every nine years when the bark fully regrows, for up to 300 years. At its eventual end of life, just cut out the metal snaps and compost everything else. The many different sizes available ensure you can find something for every shape and size of laptop.

17. Newspaper Colored Pencils

School isn't all reading, writing, and arithmetic. Sometimes it's fun and we want sustainable art supplies to keep that fun, clean and healthy. Recycled newspaper makes for the best eco-friendly pencils (colored or not) which are great for two reasons: 1) they reduce landfill waste by putting newspaper to a second use; 2) they don't promote deforestation.

The tightly coiled newspaper held together by earth safe adhesive is sturdy to hold, while the non-toxic colored graphite goes on smooth and extra dark (which they claim provides double the life of traditional colored pencils).

18. Zero Waste Crayons

Conventional crayons are made of petroleum-based paraffin and are tinted with chemical dyes. To that, we say 'time to color outside the lines'. Earth Grown crayons are made of organic, vegan soy wax and mineral pigments that have been certified non-toxic by related third party organizations. All ingredients are sourced from farms and have been grown without pesticides or herbicides. They're also packaged in an uncoated cardboard box with shredded cardboard filling which is 100% compostable.

19. Art Drawing Pad

The Eco Art drawing pad is comprised of FSC and Rainforest Alliance-certified post-consumer agricultural waste. Specifically, it's made from pinzotes, the discarded stalks from banana trees. Each sheet is solid enough to be suitable for paints, markers, and crayons alike.

Environmental Shopping Guide for Paper Products

Sustainable purchasing is about including social, environmental, financial and performance factors in a systematic way. It involves thinking about the reasons for using the product (the service) and assessing how these services could be best met. If a product is needed, sustainable purchasing involves considering how products are made, what they are made of, where they come from and how they will be used and disposed.

Wherever possible RECOMENDED products that employ a combination of characteristics listed in the left hand column, and NOT-RECOMENDED products that demonstrate characteristic in the right-hand column.

RECOMENDED	NOT-RECOMENDED
• International Ecolabel certified • High post-consumer recycled fibre content • Non-wood • Chlorine free • Paper that is less bright	• Not Ecolabel certified • Long distance transport • Unsustainably harvested wood resources

A Simple Sustainable Plan

A	Reduce paper use
B	Use EcoLabel Certified Products
C	Choose High Post-Consumer Recycled Content
D	Choose Non-Wood (Tree-free) Fibres
E	Choose Less Transportation
F	Use Sustainably Harvested Wood Fibre
G	Choose Chlorine-Free Paper
H	Select Paper with Appropriate Brightness

A: Reduce paper use

The first step toward a more sustainable paper cycle is to reduce use. Using less paper saves money and contributes to sustainability by mitigating the environmental impact of production and use. The average North American now uses 227 Kilograms of paper per year, more than double the global average. Consuming less paper reduces the impacts of paper production and the associated energy use from operating printers and copiers. Both of these processes are known to have negative impacts for sustainability and should be minimized.

Strategies for reducing paper use include:

• Electronically archiving instead of printing non-critical documents
• Sharing and reviewing document drafts electronically
• Purchasing a duplex printer/photocopier and selecting double-sided printing as the default
• Re-using paper that is already printed on one side for draft copies

---

Even if paper use declines in industrialized countries, developing nations will continue to increase their consumption as they gain access to more information and technology. Many countries currently have insufficient paper to fulfill basic education needs. It is therefore essential that paper consumption be closely monitored and restrained so that the resource, and the benefits it provides, can be more equally distributed to meet future needs.

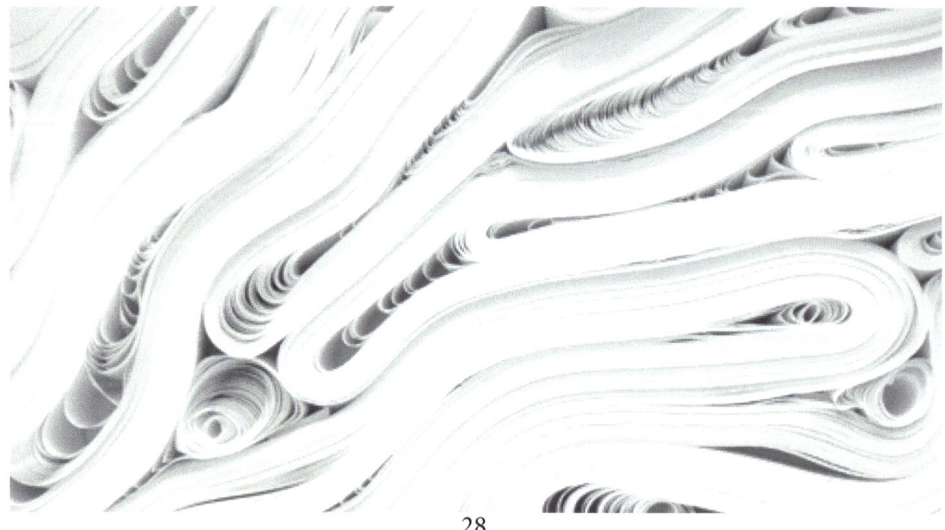

B: Use EcoLabel Certified Products

Environmental Choice certified (eg. FSC certified International Environ-mental Labelling Series, Vol.6, Page: 29) paper products have met the re-quired standards regarding noxious emissions to water, wastewater discharge levels, use of recycled content, solid waste volume, potential contribution to acid rain and climate change, energy use and forestry and habitat conser-vation. This widely respected sustainability rating provides an easy way of distinguishing genuinely green products from their competitors.

C: Choose High Post-Consumer Recycled Content

As opposed to virgin fibres, post-consumer recycled fibres have been re-covered from paper products already "consumed" by an end user. The use of these recycled fibres directly reduces the use of forest resources, in turn mitigating the associated habitat destruction, loss of top soil and other forms of ecosystem damage.

Recycling one tonne of paper:

• Saves up to 31 trees, 4,000 kWh of energy, 1.7 barrels (270 litres) of oil, 10.2 million Btu's of energy, 26,000 litres of water and 3.5 cubic metres of landfill space

• Burning that same tonne of paper would generate about 750 kilograms of carbon dioxide

• Recycling paper saves 65% of the energy needed to make new paper and also re-duces water pollution by 35% and air pollution by 74%

D: Choose Non-Wood (Tree-free) Fibres

Non-wood plant fibres do not need to be bleached with chlorine to be lightened, consume less energy when being processed, release fewer greenhouse gases in the production process and has less harmful water discharge. Crops grown specifically for the purpose of paper production can include Kanaf, jute, flax and hemp. Certain agricultural residues, such as wheat stalks and sugar cane bagasse, can also be processed into non-wood paper. When choosing non-wood fibres, preference should be given to those that are organically and sustainably grown. This eliminates the use of synthetic fertilizers, herbicides and pesticides, reducing the associated ecological and human health impacts.

E: Choose Less Transportation

The proximity of where the fibres are harvested, where the final products are produced and your own location has a significant impact on the sustainability of paper production. Growing, producing and buying locally will reduce emissions from fossil fuels. Transportation may have to be weighed against some of the other desired characteristics. More information regarding sustainable methods of transportation is available in the Transportation Guide.

F: Use Sustainably Harvested Wood Fibre

When using wood-based fibres, it is important to consider how the forest resources from which the paper was derived are managed and harvested. Preference should be given to companies that practice sustainable forestry techniques. Third party organizations such as the Forest Stewardship Council (FSC, Vol.6 Page 29) certify the harvesting and management of forestry resources to ensure long-term sustainability.

G: Choose Chlorine-Free Paper

To reduce the potential risks associated with chlorine compounds, a number of paper manufacturers are switching to chlorine-free compounds for whitening paper. Alternative bleaching agents include: oxygen, hydrogen peroxide or ozone treatments. Paper products often identify the bleaching method used for processing pulp. Paper products processed with derivatives of chlorine produce fewer dioxins than regular chlorine. This process is described as elemental chlorine free (ECF). Products bleached with no chlorine and no chlorine derivatives are sometimes referred to as totally chlorine free (TCF) or process chlorine free.

H: Select Paper with Appropriate Brightness

The brightness of paper is largely a function of the chemicals used in the pulp and/or the amount of recycled fibres used in the paper. Selecting less bright paper can reduce overall impacts. The function or use of the paper influences how bright the paper needs to be. For example, copy paper is generally not used for publicity or advertising. When the content, rather than the appearance of the paper matters, the whiteness is irrelevant as long as the text is legible. It is important to appropriately match the paper to its purpose.

How can we make stationery eco friendly? Making your supplies & stationery stockpile more sustainable

- Make sure your paper has been sourced sustainably.
- Print double-sided and black & white.
- Cork noticeboards.
- Swap pens for pencils where possible.
- Reuse and recycle boxes and packaging.

1) For example, One of the largest pencil brand in the world, has a pioneering forestation project in Brazil and Colombia where two million trees are planted every year.
A) True
B) False
ANSWER:

2) Second-hand online school supplies like books, graphing calculators, and other technology have a big positive social and environmental impact. They reduce carbon emissions, save lots of resources, water, and energy.
A) True
B) False
ANSWER:

3) There are many eco-friendly school supplies from Canada.
A) True
B) False
ANSWER:

4) These 5 or 8 tab sets are made out of %85 post-consumer and %15 post-industrial recycled content. Unlike many recycled paper products that get shipped to Asia and back again, the waste is collected and remade entirely in the USA.
A) True
B) False
ANSWER:

5) The Eco Art drawing pad is comprised of FSC and Rainforest Alliance-certified post-consumer agricultural waste.
A) True
B) False
ANSWER:

6) Describe ‹Decomposition Books›The best sustainable notebooks we found are different type of Decomposition books. These lovely college-ruled decomposition books are an excellent non-toxic and compostable note-taking solution.
A) True
B) False
ANSWER:

7) The best sustainable notebooks we found are different type of _____ books.
A) Decomposition
B) European
C) wooden
D) colored
ANSWER:

8) here are a few strategies for sustainable, low or zero waste school supplies and stationery:
A) Use what you already have
B) Scrounge up loose pens and forgotten notebooks
C) consider donating any school supplies
D) All of them
ANSWER:

9) Sustainable FSC certified wooden pencils are zero waste and have a non-toxic.
A) True
B) False
ANSWER:

10) Consuming less paper reduces the impacts of paper production and the associated energy use from operating printers and copiers
A) True
B) False
ANSWER:

11) These lovely college-ruled decomposition books are an excellent non-toxic and compostable note-taking solution.
A) True
B) False
ANSWER:

12) _____ programs authorize the use of environmental logos on products.
A) Ecolabel
B) Systematic
C) New
D) All of them
ANSWER:

13) Strategies for reducing paper use include:
A) Electronically archiving instead of printing non-critical documents
B) Sharing and reviewing document drafts electronically
C) Purchasing a duplex printer/photocopier and selecting double-sided printing as the default
D) Re-using paper that is already printed on one side for draft copies
E) All of Them
ANSWER:

14) What is a simple first step to take stationery? Eco stationery.
A) True
B) False
ANSWER:

15) What is a more sustainable paper cycle? Reduce use.
A) True
B) False
ANSWER:

16) To reduce the potential risks associated with chlorine compounds, a number of paper manufacturers are switching to chlorine-free compounds for whitening paper
A) True
B) False
ANSWER:

17) What is the term referring to all kinds of green stationery? Eco-friendly pens.
A) True
B) False
ANSWER:

18) What kind of stationery is eco friendly? recycled and sustainable
A) True
B) False
ANSWER:

19) What is the purpose of Eco Friendly Stationery? recycled
A) True
B) False
ANSWER:

20) Sustainable stationery is also more likely to use renewable raw materials such as wood and eco plastics, rather than single-use plastics made from fossil fuels.
A) True
B) False
ANSWER:

21) Best option available to purchase a printer is DUPLEX, double sided printing
A) True
B) False
ANSWER:

22) What is one of the reasons why many countries are not able to fulfill basic education needs?
A) Tablet
B) Paper
C) Computer
D) Whiteboard
ANSWER:

23) Sharpen your eco-friendly pencils with this double hole eco-friendly pencil sharpener made of sustainably sourced bamboo and recycled stainless steel.
A) True
B) False
ANSWER:

24) The dual-sided eraser made of all-natural rubber latex (to erase pencil) and natural silica sand (to erase ink and some markers). One zero waste eraser for all your mistakes.
A) True
B) False
ANSWER:

25) Now you need something to store all those eco-conscious goodies in, If you don't have a ditty bag lying around the house check out this line of eco-friendly school supplies from Canada. Their %100 organic cotton zippered pencil bags are available in tons of colors.
A) True
B) False
ANSWER:

Bibliography:

Amberg, N.; Magda, R. Environmental Pollution and Sustainability or the Impact of the Environmentally Conscious Measures of International Cosmetic Companies on Purchasing Organic Cosmetics. Visegrad J. Bioecon. Sustain. Dev. 2018, 1, 23.

Asadi, J., "International Environmental Labelling, Economic Consequencies, Export Magazine, July 2001

Asadi, J. 2008. Mobile Phone as management systems tools, ISO Magazine, Vol.8, No.1

Asadi, J., Eco-Labelling Standards, National Standard Magazine, Sep. 2004.

Barbieux, D.; Padula, A.D. Paths and Challenges of New Technologies: The Case of Nanotechnology-Based Cosmetics Development in Brazil. Adm. Sci. 2018, 8, 16.

Advanced Engineering and Applied Sciences: An International Journal 2014; 4(3): 26-28

Berolzheimer, C. (2006). Pencils: An Environmental Profile.

Chemical Week, 1999. Europe's Beef Ban Tests Precautionary Principle. (August 11).

Chaudri, S.K.; Jain, N.K. History of Cosmetics. Asian J. Pharm. 2009, 7–9, 164–167.

CHOI, J.P. Brand Extension as Informational Leverage. Review of Eco- nomic Studies, Vol. 65 (1998), pp. 655-669.

Conway, G. 2000. Genetically modified crops: risks and promise.

Corrado, M., (1989), The Greening Consumer in Britain, MORI, London

Corrado, M., (1997), Green Behaviour – Sustainable Trends, Sustainable Lives?, MORI, london, accessed via countries. Manila, Asian Development Bank 33p.

Davies, Clive. Chief, Design for the Environment Program, Environmental Protection Agency. Interview. March 24, 2009.

Federal Trade Commission, "Sorting Out Green Advertising Claims." http://www.ftc.gov/bcp/edu/pubs/consumer/general/gen02.shtm (March 26, 2009, March 27, 2009)

Ooyen, Carla. Research Manager with Nutrition Business Journal. Personal correspondence. March 19, 2009.

Tekin, Jenn. Marketing Manager with Packaged Facts & SBI. Personal correspondence. March 17, 2009.

University of California - Berkeley. http://berkeley.edu/news/media/releases/2006/05/22_householdchemicals.shtml (March 26, 2009)

U.S. Department of Health and Human Services, Household Products Database.http://householdproducts.nlm.nih.gov/cgi-bin/household/prodtree?prodcat=Inside+the+Home (March 17,

Women's Voices of the Earth, "Household Cleaning Products and Effects on Human Health."http://www.womenandenvironment.org/campaignsandprograms/SafeCleaning/safecleaninghealth (March 17, 2009)

EMONS, W. Credence Goods Monopolists. International Journal of In- dustrial Organization, Vol. 19 (2001), pp. 375-389.

European Union official website: https://ec.europa.eu/info/about-european-commission/contact_en

Feenstra, R.C. "Exact Hedonic Price Indexes," Review of Economics and Statistics 77 (1995): 634-653.

Feenstra, R.C., and J.A. Levinsohn. "Estimating Markups and Market Conduct with Multidimensional Product Attributes," Review of Economic Studies (62 (1995): 19-52.

ForestEthics. (n.d.). Back to School Report Card.

Forest Stewardship Council: "Principles and criteria for forest stewardship" Document 1.2: <http://www.fscoax.org>

Forsyth, K. 1999. Will consumers pay more for certified wood products? Journal of Forestry 97 (2) : 18-22.

ForestChoice #2 (2014, January 1). ForestChoice #2 Graphite Pencils (12 Pack).

Francois, C., Harris, B. (2014, November 2). How are Mechanical Pencils Made?.

Freeman, A. M III. The Measurement of Environmental and Resource Values. Theory and Methods. Washington D.C.: Resource for the Future, 1993.

Friends of the Earth, 1993. Timber certification and eco-labeling. London, FOE:

Geetha Margret Soundri, "Ecofriendly Antimicrobial Finishing of Textiles Using Natural Extract", Journal of International Academic Research For Multidisciplinary, ISSN: 2320 – 5083, 2014, Vol 2.

Graves, P., J.C. Murdoch, M.A. Thayer, and D. Waldman. "The Robustness of Hedonic Price Estimation: Urban Air Quality," Land Economics 64(1988): 220-233.

Halvorsen, R. and R. Palmquist. "The Interpretation of Dummy Variables in Semilogarithmic Equations." American Economic Review 70:474-75 (1980).

Henderson D. (2008). Opportunity Cost." The Concise Encyclopedia of Economics.

How It's Made. (2009, Nov 17). How It's Made Graphite Pencil Leads [video file].

Imhoff, Dan. "Growing Pains: Organic Cotton Tests the Fibre of Growers and Manufacturers Alike," reprinted on Simple Life's web page (simplelife.com), but first printed by Farmer to Farmer, December 1995.

Incomplete Consumer Information in Laboratory Markets. Journal of Environmental labeling.

ISO 14020, ISO 14021,ISO 14024,ISO 14025, International Organization for Standardization.

Kennedy, P.E. "Estimation with Correctly Interpreted Dummy Variables in Semilogarithmic Equations," American Economic Review 71: 801 (1981).

Kirchho®, S., (2000), Green Business and Blue Angels.

Kraus, Jeff. Lab Technician at the North Carolina School of Textiles.

Labeling Issues, Policies and Practices Worldwide.

Lamport, L. 1998. The cast of (timber) certifiers: who are they? International J. Ecoforestry 11(4): 118-122.

Large Scale impoverishment of Amazonian forests by logging and fire. 1999.

Lathrop, K.W. and Centner, T.J. 1998. Eco-labeling and ISO 14000: An analysis of US regulatory systems and issues concerning adoption of type II standards. Environmental

Lee, J. et al. 1996. Trade related environmental measures; sizing and comparing impacts.

Lehtonen, Markku. 1997. Criteria in Environmental Labeling: A comparative Analysis on Environmental Criteria in Selected Labeling Schemes. Geneva, UNEP. 148p.

LIEBI, T. Trusting Labels: A Matter of Numbers? Working Paper Uni versity of Bern, No. 0201 (2002).

Lindstrom, T. 1999. Forest Certification: The View from Europe's NIPFs. Journal of Forestry 97(3): 25-31. London

Losey, J.E., Rayor, L.S. & Carter, M.E. 1999. Transgenic pollen harms monarch larvae. Nature 399 20 May): p.214.

Mattel Ever After High Cedar Wood Doll. (2014, July 3).

Management 22 (2) : 163-172.

Mattoo, A. and H. V. Singh, (1994), Eco-Labelling: Policy Considera-Michaels, R. G., and V. K. Smith. "Market Segmentation And Valuing Amenities With Hedonic Models: The Case Of Hazardous Waste Sites," Journal of Urban Economics, 1990 28(2), 223-242.

Nicholson-Lord, D., (1993) 'Tis the Season to be Green, The Independent, 20 December

Nuttall, N., (1993), Shoppers can cross green products off their lists, The Times, 3 July

OCDE/GD(97)105. Paris, OECD. 81p.

OECD. "Ec-labelling: Actual Effects of Selected Programmes," OCDE/GD (97) 105, 1997, Paris. (available on line at http://www.oecd.org/env/eco/books.htm#trademono)

OECD. 1997a. Case study on eco-labeling schemes. Paris, OECD (30 Dec):

OECD. 1997b. Eco-labeling: Actual Effects of Selected Programs.

Osborne, L. "Market Structure, Hedonic Models, and the Valuation of Environmental Amenities." Unpublished Ph.D. dissertation. North Carolina State University, 1995.

Osborne, L., and V. K. Smith. "Environmental Amenities, Product Differentiation, and market Power," Mimeo, 1997.

Ozanne, L.K. and Vlosky, R.P. 1996. Wood products environmental certification: the United States perspective". Forestry Chronicle 72 (2) : 157-165.

Palmquist, R. B., F. M. Roka, and T.Vukina. "Hog Operations, Environmental Effects, and Residential Property Values," Land Economics 73(1), (1997): 114-24.

Palmquist, R.B. "Hedonic Methods," in J.B Braden and C.D. Kolstad, eds. Measuring the Demand for Environmental Improvement. Amsterdam, NL: Elsevier, 1991.

Paper Mate. (2014). Paper Mate Recycled.

Pento, T. 1997. Implementation of Public Green Procurement Programs (22-31) in Greener Purchasing: Opportunities and Innovations. Sheffield, Greenleaf Publ. 325 p.

Perloff, J. "Industrial Organization Lecture Notes," Mimeo. University of California at Berkeley (1985).

Plant, C. and Plant, J. 1991. Green business: hope or hoax? Philadelphia, New Society Publishers 136 p.

Pencil Making Today (2014, January 1). Pencil Making Today: How to Make a Pencil in 10 Steps.

Polak, J. and Bergholm, K. 1997. Eco-labeling and trade: a cooperative approach (Jan.): Policy in a Green Market. Environmental and Resource Economics 22, 419-

Poore, M.E.D. et al. 1989. No timber without trees. London, Earthscan. 352p.

Raff, D. M.G., and M. Trajtenberg. "Quality-Adjusted Prices for the American Automobile Industry: 1906-1940." NBER Working Paper Series, Working Paper No. 5035, February 1995.

Roberts, J. T. 1998. Emerging global environment standards: prospects and perils. Journal of Developing Societies 14 (1): 144-163.

Rosen, S., "Hedonic Prices and Implicit Markets: Product Differentiation in Pure Competition." Journal of Political Economy. 82: 34-55 (1974).

Ross, B. 1997. Eco-friendly procurement training course for UN HCR. : 126 p.

Ryan, S., and Skipworth, M., (1993), Consumers turn their backs on green revolution, The Times, 4 April

Salzman, J. 1997. Informing the Green Consumer: The Debate over the Use and Abuse of Environmental Labels. Journal of Industrial Ecology 1 (2): 11-22.

Sanders, W. 1997. Environmentally Preferable Purchasing: The US Experience (946-960) in Greener Purchasing: Opportunities and Innovations. Sheffield, Greenleaf Publ. 325p.

Sayre, D. 1996. Inside ISO 14000: The competitive advantage of environmental management. Delray Beach FL., St. Lucie Press. 232p.

Suzuki, D. (2014, January 1). PEG Compounds and their contaminants

SHAPIRO, C. Premiums for High Quality Products as Returns to Reputa- tion. Quarterly Journal of Economics, Vol. 98, No. 4 (1983), pp. 659-680.

Stillwell, M. and van Dyke, B. 1999. An activists handbook on genetically modified organisms and the WTO. Washington DC., The Consumer's Choice Council: 20 p.

Semenzato, A.; Costantini, A.; Meloni, M.; Maramaldi, G.; Meneghin, M.; Baratto, G. Formulating O/W Emulsions with Plant-Based Actives: A Stability Challenge for an Eective Product. Cosmetics 2018, 5, 59.

Sources of Plastics (2014, January 1). Sources of Plastics.

Singh, S. (2008, March 6). Paraffin wax.

Saint Jean Carbon. (n.d.). Sri Lankan Graphite.

Teisl, M. F., B. Roe, and R. L. Hicks. "Can Eco-labels tune a market? Evidence from dolphin-safe labeling," Presented paper at the 1997 American Agricultural Economics Association Meetings, Toronto.

Tollefson, Jennifer E. (2008). Calocedrus Decurrens.

THE GERSEN, C. Psychological Determinants of Paying Attention to Eco- Labels in Purchase Decisions: Model Development and Multinational Vali- dation. Journal of Consumer Policy, Vol. 23, No. 4 (2000), pp. 285-313.

Tibor, T. and Feldman, I. 1995. ISO 14000: a guide to the new environmental management standards. Burr Ridge Ill., Irwin Professional Publ. 250 p.

TU.S. Energy Information Administration, What is U.S. Electricity Generation by Energy Source?, Retrieved From: https://www.eia.gov/tools/faqs/faq.php?id=427&t=3

U.S. Energy Information Administration, Biomass Explained, Retrieved From: https://www.eia.gov/energyexplained/?page=biomass_home

U.S. Environmental Protection Agency, National Water Quality Fact Inventory: 1990 Report to Congress. EPA 503-9-92-006, Apr. 1992.

UK Eco-labelling Board website, accessed via http://www.ecosite.co.uk/Ecolabel-UK/

US Environmental Protection Agency (EPA742-R-99-001): 40 p. <www.epa.gov/opptintr/epp>

US EPA, 1993. Determinants of effectiveness for environmental certification and labeling programs. Washington, D.C., US Environmental Protect

US EPA, 1993. Status report on the use of environmental labels worldwide. Washington, D.C., US Environmental Protection Agency (742-R-93-001 September).

US EPA, 1993. The use of life-cycle assessment in environmental labeling. Washington, D.C., US Environmental Protection Agency (742-R-93-003 September).

US EPA, 1998. Environmental labeling: issues, policies, and practices worldwide. Washington DC., Environmental Protection Agency, Pollution Prevention Division Prepared by Abt

US EPA, 1999. Comprehensive procurement guidelines (CPG) program. Washington, D.C., US Environmental Protection Agency: <www.epa.gov/cpg>

US EPA, 1999. Environmentally preferable purchasing program: Private sector pioneers: How companies are incorporating environmentally preferable purchases. Washington University of Saskatchewan, Sustainable purchasing guide.

USG, 1993. Federal acquisition, recycling, and waste prevention. Washington DC., Executive Order: (20 October).

USG, 1998. Greening the government through waste prevention, recycling, and federal acquisition. Washington, D.C., Executive Order 13101 (September).

Kijjoa, A.; Sawangwong, P. Drugs and Cosmetics from the Sea. Mar. Drugs 2004, 2, 73–82. [CrossRef]

Wang, J.; Pan, L.; Wu, S.; Lu, L.; Xu, Y.; Zhu, Y.; Guo, M.; Zhuang, S. Recent Advances on Endocrine Disrupting Eects of UV Filters. Int. J. Environ. Res. Public Health 2016, 13, 782.

Bilal, A.I.; Tilahun, Z.; Shimels, T.; Gelan, Y.B.; Osman, E.D. Cosmetics Utilization Practice in Jigjiga Town, Eastern Ethiopia: A Community Based Cross-Sectional Study. Cosmetics 2016, 3, 40.

Ting, C.T.; Hsieh, C.M.; Chang, H.-P.; Chen, H.-S. Environmental Consciousness and Green Customer Behavior: The Moderating Roles of Incentive Mechanisms. Sustainability 2019, 11, 819.

Chen, K.; Deng, T. Research on the Green Purchase Intentions from the Perspective of Product Knowledge. Sustainability 2016, 8, 943.

Wang, H.; Ma, B.; Bai, R. How Does Green Product Knowledge Eectively Promote Green Purchase Intention? Sustainability 2019, 11, 1193.

Nguyen, T.T.H.; Yang, Z.; Nguyen, N.; Johnson, L.W.; Cao, T.K. Greenwash and Green Purchase Intention: The Mediating Role of Green Skepticism. Sustainability 2019, 11, 2653.

Cinelli, P.; Coltelli, M.B.; Signori, F.; Morganti, P.; Lazzeri, A. Cosmetic Packaging to Save the Environment: Future Perspectives. Cosmetics 2019, 6, 26.

Eixarch, H.; Wyness, L.; Siband, M. The Regulation of Personalized Cosmetics in the EU. Cosmetics 2019, 6, 29.

CANADA BRONZE BEAVER BADGE

Participate in our Online Classes to earn these exclusive digital badges!
www.toptenaward.org

Design & Development by:

Tara Asadi

CANADA GOLD BEAVER BADGE

Participate in our Online Classes to earn these exclusive digital badges!

Design & Development by:

Tara Asadi

Environmental Lifestyle Guide

For Grade 9

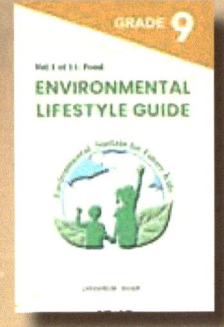

For Grade 10

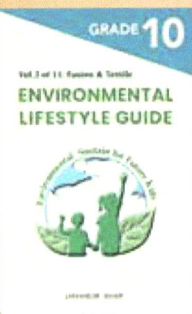

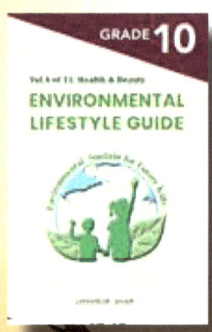

Plus Online Certification Tests via:
https://toptenaward.org

Standard Text Books

For Grade 11

For Grade 12

 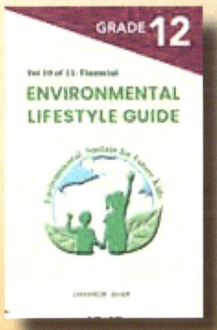 

**Environmental Lifestyle Guide
Standard Text Book**
For Students Grade 9 to 12
Available in more than
39,000 Bookstores
all over the globe.
https://ecofriendlyeducation.com

Cooperation by:
Top Ten Award International Network
&
Environmental Sustain for Future Kids

www.ingramcontent.com/pod-product-compliance
Lightning Source LLC
Chambersburg PA
CBHW040858120626
46551CB00001B/77